Contents

How to Use This Book   2

Pre-assessment Activities   4

Section One: Learning Numbers   10
Teaching Tips   10
Identifying Written Numerals (1–5)   11
Identifying Written Numerals (6–10)   12
Matching Numbers with Quantities (1–5)   13
Matching Numbers with Quantities (6–10)   14
Post-assessment Activities   15

Section Two: Counting   16
Teaching Tips   16
Counting on a Number Line   17
Counting How Many in a Set   18
Counting and Comparing: More   19
Counting and Comparing: Less   20
Post-assessment Activities   21

Section Three: More Counting   22
Teaching Tips   22
Ordinal Numbers   23
Place Value   24
Counting Up to 20   25
Counting Up to 30   26
Post-assessment Activities   27

Section Four: Addition   28
Teaching Tips   28
Adding 1 to Numbers (1–5)   29
Adding 1 to Numbers (6–9)   30
Adding Two Numbers (Up to 5)   31
Adding Two Numbers (Up to 10)   32
Post-assessment Activities   33

Section Five: Subtraction   34
Teaching Tips   34
Subtracting 1 from Numbers (1–5)   35
Subtracting 1 from Numbers (6–10)   36
Subtracting Two Numbers (Up to 5)   37
Subtracting Two Numbers (Up to 10)   38
Post-assessment Activities   39

Section Six: Money   40
Teaching Tips   40
Learning About Pennies   41
Learning About Nickels   42
Learning About Dimes   43
Learning About Quarters   44
Post-assessment Activities   45

Answer Key   46

How to Use This Book

The goal of *Numbers and Operations* is to increase the learners' proficiency in numbers and mathematical operations at the kindergarten level. The subject matter featured in these activities has been chosen based on curriculum used in schools nationwide. The activities and skills follow a sampling of the National Council of Teachers of Mathematics (NCTM) standards with a focus on science and social studies topics. The activities have been designed to capture the learners' interests by presenting material in a fun and exciting way.

Numbers and Operations is organized into six sections: Learning Numbers, Counting, More Counting, Addition, Subtraction, and Money. Each section focuses on an important aspect of numbers and mathematical operations, offering easy-to-understand skill definitions and activity directions.

✏️ Learning Numbers
Learners will practice identifying numerals and number words up to 10. They will count familiar objects with an understanding that numbers can represent quantities.

✏️ Counting
Number lines are introduced in this section. Learners will count and recognize "how many" in sets of objects. Other activities explore the meanings of the words "more" and "less" in relation to groups of objects.

2

▭▶More Counting
In this section, learners explore more advanced number concepts, including the place value system. The connection between cardinal and ordinal numbers is presented in the context of the calendar. Learners will also practice counting quantities up to 30.

▭▶Addition
Learners will be guided into the process of addition by first learning to add 1 to a number. They will also receive practice with adding different combinations of numbers up to 10. Familiar objects are included in activities that allow learners to practice different methods of computation.

▭▶Subtraction
Subtraction is presented first through taking away 1 from a number and then by subtracting other numbers. Visual representations are provided for learners as they subtract different combinations of numbers up to 10.

▭▶Money
The concept of money is introduced through photographs of pennies, nickels, dimes, and quarters. Learners will be taught to discriminate between a penny, nickel, dime, and quarter. They will also learn the value of each coin.

3

Name _____

Number Match

We can match numbers and number words.

Directions: Look at each number below. Draw a line from each number to the word that matches it.

1	three
2	one
3	five
4	two
5	four

4

Name _____

How Many People?

We can count how many are in a group.

✏️ **Directions: Count how many people are in each group.
Write the number on the line.**

1.  _____

2.  _____

3.  _____

4.  _____

5.  _____

Name _____

Missing Numbers

We can count and write numbers up to 30.

✏️ **Directions: Look at the chart below. Fill in the blank boxes with the missing numbers.**

1		3	4	5
6	7		9	10
	12	13	14	15
16	17		19	20
21		23	24	25
26	27		29	30

Name _____

A Camping Trip

Adding two numbers gives us a new number.

✏️ **Directions: My family went on a camping trip. We all took things we needed. Read each example. Answer the question.**

1. Mom took 4 fishing poles. Dad took 1 more fishing pole. How many fishing poles were there? _____

4   1

2. Dad took 8 pillows. I took 1 more pillow. How many pillows were there? _____

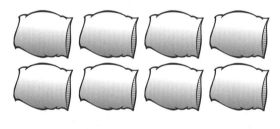

8   1

3. Mom took 4 hats. Mary took 3 more hats. How many hats were there? _____

4   3

7

Name _____

The Lemonade Sale

We can subtract to find out how many are left.

> **Directions: We had a lemonade sale. Some people made the lemonade. Some people sold the lemonade. Read each example. Answer the questions.**

1. Dave had 5 lemons. He used 1 lemon. How many were left?

   _____ lemons

2. Sal had 8 lemons. He used 4 lemons. How many were left?

   _____ lemons

3. Kay had 7 cups of lemonade. She sold 5 cups. How many were left?

   _____ cups

Name _____

Count the Coins

Coins look different and have different values.

> **Directions: Count the number of pennies in each row. Write the number on the line.**

_____ pennies

_____ pennies

> **Directions: Look at the coins below. Draw a line from each coin to its value.**

10¢

25¢

5¢

Teaching Tips...

For *Learning Numbers* (pp. 11–15)

Background

• Using numerals and number words is an important skill in mathematics and language arts. Pictures of familiar objects reinforce the idea that mathematics is a part of daily life.

Homework Helper

• Find ten similar objects that are familiar to the learner. Group a number of the objects. Ask the learner to draw the objects and write the number and number word below the picture. Repeat this activity with numbers up to 10.

Research-based Activity

• Give learners a section of newspaper. Have them find and circle numbers on several pages. Guide learners in discussing why numbers are important in our world.

Test Prep

• Learners at this level are introduced to activities that will prepare them for the testing format they will encounter on standardized tests beginning in the higher elementary grades. The test preparation skills covered in this section include matching terms, providing responses to questions, and reading and following written directions.

Different Audiences

• To adapt this section to an accelerated learner, create matching columns for numbers and number words 11–20 (see p. 15). Ask the learner to draw a line from the number to the number word that matches it.

Name _____

The Names of Numbers

Numbers help us count how many. Numbers can be written in different ways.

Directions: Choose the word in the box that matches each number. Write the word next to the number.

one   two   three   four   five

2 _____

5 _____

3 _____

1 _____

4 _____

We use numbers to tell people where we live. What is the number on the building where you live?

Name _____

More Number Names

We can use both numbers and number words.

**Directions:** Choose the word in the box that matches each number. Write the word next to the number.

six	seven	eight	nine	ten

10 _____

7 _____

8 _____

9 _____

6 _____

FUN FACT

There are ten numerals we use to make up all numbers: 0, 1, 2, 3, 4, 5, 6, 7, 8, 9.

12

Name _____

In the Garden

Numbers tell us how many are in a group.

Directions: A garden is a place where plants grow. You can grow flowers in a garden. Look at the numbers on the left. Circle the group of flowers in each row that matches the number.

1		
2		
3		
4		
5		

FUN FACT

Flowers can be many different shapes and colors.

Name _____

How Many Apples?

Numbers tell us how many are in a group.

Directions: Apples grow on apple trees. Look at the number on the left. Draw that number of apples next to it.

Example:

6

7

8

9

10

You can use apples
to make an apple pie!

14

Name _____

Skill Check—Learning Numbers

✏️ **Directions:** Draw a line from the number on the left to the number word that matches it.

1   seven

3   four

4   one

7   nine

9   three

✏️ **Directions:** Look at the numbers on the left. Circle the group in each row that matches the number.

2

7

Background

• Number lines and number comparison help learners to understand the relationships between numbers. Counting recognizable objects reinforces the connection between numbers and learners' lives.

Homework Helper

• Ask the learner to pick a book about animals. For several pages, ask the learner to count the animals, write the number on a sticky note, and stick the note to the page. Ask the learner to compare two pages. The learner should identify which page has *more* animals and which page has *less* animals.

Research-based Activity

• Help learners research a zoo on the Internet or with available materials. Assist them with finding the number of bears and giraffes in the zoo. Ask learners to draw the number of each kind of animal. Have them label the animal and number.

Test Prep

• Learners at this level are introduced to activities that will prepare them for the testing format they will encounter on standardized tests beginning in the higher elementary grades. The test preparation skills covered in this section include one-to-one correspondence, analyzing pictures for information, and following written directions.

Different Audiences

• To adapt this section to a special needs learner, find a number of similar objects (blocks, pencils, etc.). Divide the objects into two groups of different number. Ask the learner which group has more and which group has less. Vary the amounts.

Name _____

Number Lines

We can use a number line to help us count.

➡️ **Directions: Look at the number lines below. Fill in the missing numbers.**

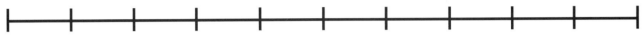

0　1　2　___　4　5　6　___　8　___　10

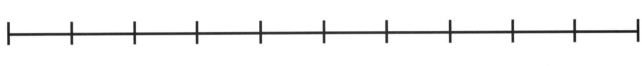

0　1　___　3　4　___　6　7　___　9　10

°F

120
110
100
90
80
70
60
50
40
30
20
10
0
-10
-20
-30
-40
-50
-60
-70

FUN FACT

A thermometer is a special kind of number line.
The numbers on a thermometer tell us how hot or cold it is.

17

Name _____

A Trip to the Zoo

We use numbers to count the things we see every day.

Directions: A zoo is a place where we can see different kinds of animals. Count how many animals are in each group. Write the number on the line.

1. _____

2. _____

3. _____

4. _____

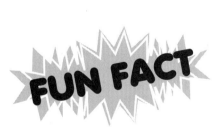

FUN FACT

A zebra is a kind of horse.

Name _____

Counting and Comparing: More

Bugs, Bugs, Bugs!

We can count to find out which group has more.

✏️ **Directions: A bug is a very small animal that has many legs. Look at the groups of bugs in each row. Circle the group that has _more_.**

Example:

1.

2.

3.

4.

Some bugs have wings that help them fly.

19

Name _____

At the Library

We can count to find out which group has less.

✏️ **Directions: A library is a place where we can find books about many different things. Look at the groups of books in each row. Circle the group that has _less_.**

Example:

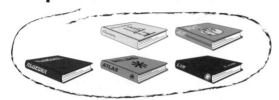 

1.

2.

3.

 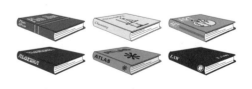

A person who works in a
library is called a librarian.

FUN FACT

Name _____

Skill Check—Counting

✏️ **Directions:** Count how many cars are in each group. Write the number on the line.

_____   _____

✏️ **Directions:** Circle the group that has <u>more</u> flowers.

✏️ **Directions:** Circle the group that has <u>less</u> apples.

Teaching Tips...

Background

• Challenging learners to think about place value, ordinal numbers, and numbers up to 30 prepares them for higher-level math skills.

Homework Helper

• On a page from an old calendar, tape pieces of paper over a few numbers. Have learners write in the missing numbers. They can lift the papers to check their work. Ask learners to count the days of the month aloud.

Research-based Activity

• Have the learner choose a book with at least 20 pages. Point out the change in place value between the page numbers 1–9 and the page numbers 10–20. Help the learner compile 10–15 sheets of paper into a book. Have them write in the page numbers.

Test Prep

• Learners at this level are introduced to activities that will prepare them for the testing format they will encounter on standardized tests beginning in the higher elementary grades. The activities include analyzing pictures and charts, reading and answering questions, using pictures to find answers, and reading and following directions.

Different Audiences

• To adapt this section to ESL learners, make a chart with three columns and seven rows. In the second column, write the numbers 1–7. In the third column, write the ordinal numbers *first* through *seventh*. Ask learners to say each ordinal number in their native language. Write those numbers in the first column. Have learners read the chart from left to right, saying the ordinal number in their native language, the numeral, and the English ordinal number.

TEACHING TIPS

22

Name _____

Days of the Week

We can count to show the order of things in a set. When we count to show order, we use the words first, second, third, fourth, fifth, sixth, seventh, and so on.

Directions: There are 7 days in a week. Sunday is the first day of the week. Saturday is the seventh day of the week. Look at the chart below. Use it to answer the questions.

Sunday	Monday	Tuesday	Wednesday	Thursday	Friday	Saturday
1	2	3	4	5	6	7
first	second	third	fourth	fifth	sixth	seventh

Example: What is the **sixth** day of the week? _____Friday_____

1. What is the **second** day of the week? _____

2. What is the **fifth** day of the week? _____

3. What is the **fourth** day of the week? _____

4. What is the **third** day of the week? _____

There are 52 weeks in a year.

Name _____

Giant Giraffes

When we count groups of tens and ones, we are using place value.

▷ **Directions: Read the story. Look at each number on the left. Write how many ones are in each number.**

Giraffes are tall animals with long legs and long necks. Some grow to be 18 feet tall!

In the number **18**, there is **1** group of ten and **8** ones. We show this by putting **1** in the tens place and **8** in the ones place.

Example:

18 ___1___ tens ___8___ ones

---

11 ___1___ tens _____ ones

12 ___1___ tens _____ ones

13 ___1___ tens _____ ones

14 ___1___ tens _____ ones

15 ___1___ tens _____ ones

The tallest giraffe was 20 feet tall!

Name _____

Rain

We can count 20 objects.

Directions: Rain is made of drops of water. Plants need rain to grow. People and animals need rain for water to drink. Count the raindrops in the picture. Write the number of raindrops on the line.

_____ raindrops

Rain falls from clouds in the sky.

25

Name _____

A Look at the Calendar

We can use a calendar to understand numbers up to 30.

Directions: A calendar shows us the months of the year. A calendar also shows us how many days are in a month. Look at the calendar below. Fill in the missing numbers.

Sunday	Monday	Tuesday	Wednesday	Thursday	Friday	Saturday
1	2	___	4	5	6	___
8	9	___	11	12	13	___
15	___	17	18	___	20	21
___	23	24	25	___	27	28
___	30					

Most months have 30 or 31 days.

Name _____

Skill Check—More Counting

Directions: Circle the picture that is **first**. Put an **X** on the picture that is **third**.

Directions: Fill in the missing numbers.

15   16   _____   18   19   20

20   21   22   23   _____   25

Directions: Count the number of flowers in the garden. Write the number on the line.

        _____

27

Teaching Tips...

TEACHING TIPS

Background

• An understanding of simple addition provides a foundation for all number operations. Pictures aid students in connecting groups of objects with numbers.

Homework Helper

• Present the learner with a pair of dice. First, place one die on a table with the "1" side face up. Have the learner roll the other die, adding the quantities seen on both dice. Ask the learner to repeat rolling one die several times and adding 1.

Research-based Activity

• Show learners how to use educational software that focuses on adding numbers with sums up to 10. Ask parents or older students to monitor progress.

Test Prep

• Learners at this level are introduced to activities that will prepare them for the testing format they will encounter on standardized tests beginning in the higher elementary grades. The test preparation skills covered in this section include reading and following written directions, using pictures to answer questions, and writing and choosing responses to questions.

Different Audiences

• To adapt this section to special needs learners, help them cut out 10 pictures of people from a magazine. Arrange a number of cutout people in a group. Place one cutout person apart. Ask the learners to add the group of people and the single cutout, allowing them to handle and regroup the cutouts. Repeat several times, arranging different groups of cutout people.

28

Name _____

Penguins

Adding 1 to a number makes a number that is 1 more.

Directions: Penguins are large birds. Penguins cannot fly, but they can swim! Add 1 penguin to the first set of penguins in each row. Write the total number on the line.

Example:

1   1   __2__

2   1   _____

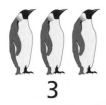

3   1   _____

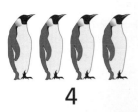 

4   1   _____

FUN FACT

Many penguins use rocks to build their nests.

29

Name _____

Terrific Turtles

*When we add numbers together, the answer is called the **sum**.*

Directions: Turtles are slow animals. They can hide their heads and legs in their shells when they are scared! Add the turtles in each row. Draw a line from each row on the left to its matching sum on the right.

Example:

🐢🐢🐢🐢🐢 **+** 🐢
5   1   **8**

🐢🐢🐢🐢🐢🐢 **+** 🐢
6   1   **10**

🐢🐢🐢🐢🐢🐢🐢 **+** 🐢
7   1   **9**

🐢🐢🐢🐢🐢🐢🐢🐢 **+** 🐢
8   1   **6**

🐢🐢🐢🐢🐢🐢🐢🐢🐢 **+** 🐢
9   1   **7**

Some turtles live on land.
Some turtles live in water.

Name _____

Lots of Birds

We can add two sets of objects.

Directions: Birds live all around us. Add the groups of birds in each example. Write the answer on the line.

1. Ann saw 2 birds. Then she saw 2 more birds. How many birds did Ann see altogether?

    2   2   _____ birds

2. Rob saw 3 birds. Then he saw 2 more birds. How many birds did Rob see altogether?

    3   2   _____ birds

3. Pam saw 2 birds. Then she saw 3 more birds. How many birds did Pam see altogether?

    2   3   _____ birds

FUN FACT

All birds have feathers and wings.

Name _____

At the Park

We can add two sets of objects with a sum up to 10.

Directions: A park is a place where you can go to play or have a picnic. Read each example. Write the answer on the line.

1. Meg saw 5 trees in the park. Then she saw 2 more trees. How many trees did Meg see altogether?

    5   2   _____

2. Jon saw 3 dogs in the park. Then he saw 3 more dogs. How many dogs did Jon see altogether?

    3   3   _____

3. Sam saw 3 flowers in the park. Then he saw 7 more flowers. How many flowers did Sam see altogether?

    3   7   _____

FUN FACT Some parks have swings!

Name _____

Skill Check—Addition

✏️ Directions: Add the number of objects in each example. Write the answer on the line.

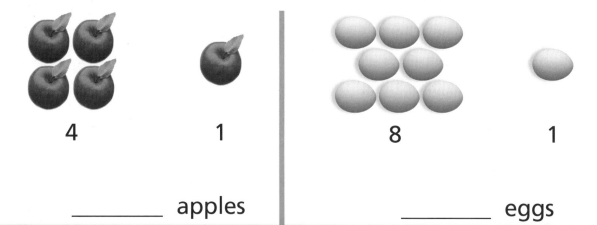

| 4 | 1 | 8 | 1 |

_____ apples   _____ eggs

✏️ Directions: Read each example. Write the answer on the line.

1. Jill saw 2 cars. Then she saw 3 more cars. How many cars did Jill see altogether?

2   3

_____ cars

2. Barb saw 5 boats. Then she saw 5 more boats. How many boats did Barb see altogether?

5   5

_____ boats

Background

• Simple subtraction problems are a foundation for more advanced operations. Familiar pictures of objects provide learners with a computational aid.

Homework Helper

• Give the learner 10 similar objects. Ask the learner to give you a number of objects and to count the remaining objects. Have the learner say the number sentence aloud (for example, "10–5=5"). Repeat this activity, varying the initial amount of objects and the number subtracted.

Research-based Activity

• Have learners ask a family member or friend a way that they use subtraction in daily life. Create simple word problems using numbers up to 10 from the learners' examples. Have learners illustrate and solve the problems. (See pp. 35–39 for examples.)

Test Prep

• Learners at this level are introduced to activities that will prepare them for the testing format they will encounter on standardized tests beginning in the higher elementary grades. The skills practiced include reading and following written directions, using illustrations to find answers, and writing the correct responses to questions.

Different Audiences

• To adapt this section to an accelerated learner, have the learner practice subtracting using numbers up to 20. For reinforcement, help the learner create flash cards with incomplete number sentences on one side (e.g., 15–1=?) and answers on the other side.

TEACHING TIPS

34

Name _____

A Birthday Party

When we subtract 1 from a number, the answer is a number that is less.

> **Directions:** Tom had a birthday party. Tom and his friends ate cupcakes at his birthday party. Count the cupcakes. Answer the questions.

1. How many cupcakes are there?

     _____ cupcakes

    Jim eats 1 cupcake. How many cupcakes are left?

     _____ cupcakes

2. How many cupcakes are there?

     _____ cupcakes

    Jan eats 1 cupcake. How many cupcakes are left?

     _____ cupcakes

3. How many cupcakes are there?

     _____ cupcakes

    Ron eats 1 cupcake. How many cupcakes are left?

     _____ cupcakes

 **FUN FACT** Your birthday is on the same day of the month every year.

Name _____

Making Art

We can subtract to find out how many are left.

Directions: Mark and Jane like to make pictures. They share many tools to make their pictures. Read each example. Write the answer on the line.

1. Mark has 7 paintbrushes. He gives 1 paintbrush to Jane. How many paintbrushes does Mark have left?

 _____ paintbrushes

2. Jane has 10 jars of paint. She gives 1 jar of paint to Mark. How many jars of paint does Jane have left?

 _____ jars of paint

3. Mark has 9 crayons. He gives 1 crayon to Jane. How many crayons does Mark have left?

 _____ crayons

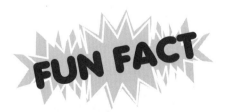

Some people make art with clay or wood.

Let's Have a Picnic

We can subtract one number from another to find how many are left.

✏️ **Directions: Ann's family had a picnic. They took many foods to eat. Read each example. Write the answer on the line.**

1. Ann's family took 5 sandwiches to the picnic. They ate 3 sandwiches. How many sandwiches were left?

     _____ sandwiches

2. Ann's family took 4 cookies to the picnic. They ate 2 cookies. How many cookies were left?

    _____ cookies

3. Ann's family took 3 apples to the picnic. They ate 2 apples. How many apples were left?

   _____ apple

{ **FUN FACT** }

Apples have seeds.

Name _____

The Bake Sale

We can subtract one number from another to find how many are left.

✏️ **Directions: Our class had a bake sale. We made treats and sold them at school. Read each example. Write the answer on the line.**

1. We made 10 cookies. We sold 7 cookies. How many cookies were left?

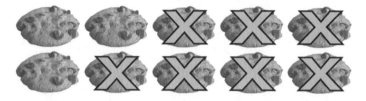

_____ cookies

2. We made 9 cakes. We sold 5 cakes. How many cakes were left?

_____ cakes

3. We made 7 pies. We sold 5 pies. How many pies were left?

_____ pies

 We can use eggs, sugar, and flour to make baked treats.

Name _____

Skill Check—Subtraction

✏️ **Directions: Jack is a baker. He needs many things to do his job. Read each example. Write the answer on the line.**

1. Jack has 5 eggs. He uses 1 egg. How many eggs are left?

_____ eggs

2. Jack has 9 bags of sugar. He uses 1 bag of sugar. How many bags of sugar are left?

_____ bags

✏️ **Directions: Meg got books from the library. Read the story below. Write the answer on the line.**

Meg has 10 books to read. She reads 4 of them. How many books does she have left to read?

_____ books

39

Teaching Tips...

Background
• This section introduces coins and their values. Learners will understand that different combinations of money can have equal values.

Homework Helper
• Give learners five each of the following coins: penny, nickel, dime, and quarter. Create several flash cards depicting items you would find in a store. Under each picture, write a value amount that corresponds with the learners' coins. Ask learners to work in pairs, exchanging cards for the correct value of coins.

Research-based Activity
• Give learners five each of the following coins: penny, nickel, dime, and quarter. Ask the learner to add the values of certain coin combinations. (For example: 3 pennies + 1 penny = 4 cents)

Test Prep
• Learners at this level are introduced to activities that will prepare them for the testing format they will encounter on standardized tests beginning in the higher elementary grades. The test preparation skills covered in this section include reading and following written directions, comparing and analyzing illustrations, and choosing or writing the correct responses to questions.

Different Audiences
• To challenge accelerated learners, ask them to review a section of the newspaper that advertises items for sale. For each item, guide the learners in deciding how many dollars, quarters, dimes, nickels, and pennies they would need. (For example: A toy is $3.15. How many dollars do we need? How many nickels?)

Name _____

Counting Pennies

We can count pennies. We know a penny has a value of 1 cent, or 1¢.

penny
1¢

✏️ **Directions: Count the pennies in each row. Circle the amount of money shown.**

Example:

                      2¢   ⟨3¢⟩

1.

      4¢   5¢

2.

              7¢   8¢

3.

             6¢   7¢

A dollar is worth 100 pennies!

41

Name _____

Counting Nickels

We can count nickels. We know a nickel has a value of 5 cents, or 5¢.

Directions: One nickel is worth 5 pennies. Count the nickels in each row. Write the number of nickels on the line.

nickel   pennies

   =

5¢   5¢

1.    _____ nickels

2.    _____ nickels

3.   _____ nickels

   =

   One dollar is worth 20 nickels.

42

Name _____

How Much Money?

We know different coins can equal 10¢. One dime has a value of 10 cents, or 10¢.

> **Directions: One dime is worth 10 pennies. One dime is also worth 2 nickels. Count how much money is shown in each example. Write the answer on the line.**

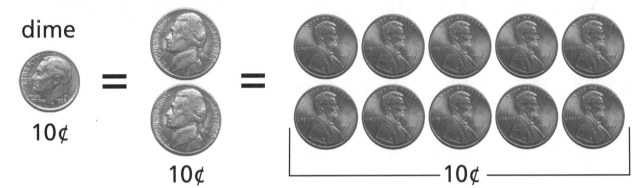

dime

10¢   =   10¢   =   10¢

1.

_____ ¢

2.

_____ ¢

3.

_____ ¢

=

FUN FACT   One dollar is worth 10 dimes.

Name _____

Counting Quarters

We can count quarters. We know a quarter has a value of 25¢.

quarter

25¢

✏️ **Directions: One quarter is worth 25¢. Count the quarters in each row. Write the number on the line.**

1.

_____ quarters

2.

_____ quarter

3.

_____ quarters

 =

One dollar is worth 4 quarters.

44

Name _____

Skill Check—Money

✏️ Directions: Look at the coins. Follow the directions below for each coin.

Put a square around each penny.	Put an X on each nickel.	Underline each dime.	Circle each quarter.

Answer Key

p. 4
1: one
2: two
3: three
4: four
5: five

p. 5
1) 2
2) 4
3) 1
4) 3
5) 5

p. 6
2, 8, 11, 18, 22, 28

p. 7
1) 5 fishing poles
2) 9 pillows
3) 7 hats

p. 8
1) 4 lemons
2) 4 lemons
3) 2 cups

p. 9
2 pennies
3 pennies
nickel: 5¢
dime: 10¢
quarter: 25¢

p. 11
2: two
5: five
3: three
1: one
4: four

p. 12
10: ten
7: seven
8: eight
9: nine
6: six

p. 13
1: 2nd group should
be circled
2: 2nd group should
be circled
3: 1st group should
be circled
4: 2nd group should
be circled
5: 1st group should
be circled

p. 14
Number of apples should
correspond with the
number shown.

p. 15
1: one
3: three
4: four
7: seven
9: nine
1st group should
be circled
1st group should
be circled

p. 17
3, 7, 9
2, 5, 8

p. 18
1) 3 zebras
2) 5 bears
3) 2 giraffes
4) 8 birds

p. 19
1) 1st group should
be circled
2) 2nd group should
be circled
3) 2nd group should
be circled
4) 1st group should
be circled

p. 20
1) 2nd group should
   be circled
2) 1st group should
   be circled
3) 2nd group should
   be circled

p. 21
3 cars
7 cars
1st group should
be circled
2nd group should
be circled

p. 23
1) Monday
2) Thursday
3) Wednesday
4) Tuesday

p. 24
1 ones
2 ones
3 ones
4 ones
5 ones

p. 25
20 raindrops

p. 26
3, 7, 10, 14, 16, 19, 22,
26, 29

p. 27
The shoe should be
circled.
There should be an X
on the sock.
missing number: 17
missing number: 24
15 flowers

p. 29
3 penguins
4 penguins
5 penguins

p. 30
7 turtles
8 turtles
9 turtles
10 turtles

p. 31
1) 4 birds
2) 5 birds
3) 5 birds

p. 32
1) 7 trees
2) 6 dogs
3) 10 flowers

p. 33
5 apples
9 eggs
1) 5 cars
2) 10 boats

p. 35
1) 5 cupcakes;
   4 cupcakes
2) 4 cupcakes;
   3 cupcakes
3) 3 cupcakes;
   2 cupcakes

p. 36
1) 6 paintbrushes
2) 9 jars of paint
3) 8 crayons

p. 37
1) 2 sandwiches
2) 2 cookies
3) 1 apple

p. 38
1) 3 cookies
2) 4 cakes
3) 2 pies

p. 39
1) 4 eggs
2) 8 bags
6 books

p. 41
1) 5¢
2) 7¢
3) 6¢

p. 42
1) 2 nickels
2) 3 nickels
3) 4 nickels

p. 43
1) 10¢
2) 10¢
3) 10¢

p. 44
1) 2 quarters
2) 1 quarter
3) 3 quarters

p. 45
Squares around 3 pennies
Xs on 3 nickels
Lines under 3 dimes
Circles around 3 quarters